MW00640036

Praying in Advent

Praying in Advent

Day by Day During Advent

Donal Neary, SJ

Pauline
BOOKS & MEDIA
Boston

Library of Congress Cataloging-in-Publication Data

Neary, Donal.
  Praying in Advent : day by day during Advent / Donal Neary.—
1st ed.
      p. cm.
  ISBN 0-8198-5945-1 (pbk.)
  1. Advent—Prayer-books and devotions—English. 2. Catho-
lic Church—Prayer-books and devotions—English. I. Title.
  BX2170.A4 N43 2003
  242'.332—dc21

                              2003004516

First edition 2002

English Edition published by The Columba Press, Blackrock,
Co Dublin

Photos: Mary Emmanuel Alves, FSP

Printed and published in the U.S.A. by Pauline Books & Media,
50 Saint Pauls Avenue, Boston, MA 02130-3491.

www.pauline.org

Pauline Books & Media is the publishing house of the Daughters
of St. Paul, an international congregation of women religious
serving the Church with the communications media.

1 2 3 4 5 6 7 8 9   11 10 09 08 07 06 05 04 03

Contents

Introduction

These pages for every day propose a simple way of praying during the weeks of Advent. The material for each day introduces you to a line or two of the Gospel reading of the day, and may serve as an invitation to read the full Gospel of the day. A reflection follows that offers some personal meaning from that day's Scripture and then a prayer that can be used in a group or personally. If you are using this book in a group, the prayer can be adapted or expanded to fit the group's needs.

A suggestion for prayerfully remembering different people then follows. This is a means of involving in our prayer people outside of ourselves, and will remind us of those we might like to pray for. For example, when the intention is *Hold in your heart today people suffering from depression*, you might remember by name those you know who suffer from depression and for whom you want to pray. You can hold a picture of them in your mind for a while, keeping them before God and asking blessings upon them. Or with the intention, *Hold in your heart today those who will not be home for Christmas*, you might name them and spend a while thinking of them in the presence of the Lord, and similarly with all the other intentions.

A prayer a day for Advent is a way of ensuring that the mystery of Christmas doesn't get lost in the bustle of Christmas preparations, and freshens our way of thinking about Christmas for another year. It also ensures that we don't cease to be amazed anew at the great event—now and then, in Bethlehem and in our own city or town—of the Incarnation of God in Jesus Christ.

—DONAL NEARY, SJ

Note: December 17 falls on different days of the third week in Advent in different calendar years. Therefore, the prayers for December 17 and following may be used in place of those days of the third week.

Gospel Mk 13:33

"Beware, keep alert, you do not know when the time will come."

Reflection

Waiting for the Messenger

People often say, "My time has come," meaning that they have no control over the time of their death. It is true that in many of the most important areas of life, we have little or no choice: our nationality, our gender, our physical make-up. Advent points out in many ways how dependent we are on God, and that God is closely involved with our lives, and how the unknowns of life make us aware of just how much of our life is lived in the context of mystery—outside our control.

Advent is also the beginning of God's dependency on us for bringing the divine Word to life. Jesus invites us in Advent to be alert to the signs of his presence in the unfolding mystery of our own lives.

Prayer

Jesus, be with us,
in time of trouble, in time of joy,
now and at the hour of death.

Intention for the Day

Hold in your heart today those who through illness have little control over their lives.

Gospel   Mt 8:11

"Many will come from the east and from the west and will eat with Abraham, Isaac and Jacob in the kingdom of heaven…."

Reflection

Inclusiveness with God

The heart of God is big, and the table of God is wide. All are included in the love of God: there are neither insiders nor outsiders. In contrast, sometimes we like to narrow down who is included and who is excluded, according to our own opinions. There may be people who feel their only place is in the back corner of the church, who feel excluded from the front seats, perhaps because of mistakes, sin, or just feeling ashamed of who they are. Religion misunderstood can sometimes encourage an "us and them" mentality.

Jesus, instead, offers an open door to his house and a chair at the head of his table to everyone—and the seat of honor to men and women others may look down on. That encourages us to offer and open our hearts to all.

Prayer

Christ of the welcome, have mercy on us.
Christ, open to all in love,
   have compassion for us.
Christ of the compassionate heart,
   make our hearts like yours.

Intention for the Day

Hold in your heart today refugees and those who seek shelter.

Gospel   Lk 10:23–24

"Blessed are the eyes that see what you see! For I tell you that many prophets and kings desired to see what you see, but did not see it, and to hear what you hear, but did not hear it."

Reflection

Seeing Jesus

Seeing Jesus was a big event in people's lives. They remembered meeting him; he was the type of person you didn't forget. Meeting him and hearing him, seeing him touch people with compassion left an impression. A feeling of well-being and love remained long after being with him.

Jesus' words go deep into the yearnings of the human heart, nourishing our good desires and challenging the not-so-good. His presence promises faithfulness and love forever. We long for this sort of meeting with him, too. We welcome into the world the astounding and faithful love of God, and we know that in Jesus, one like ourselves, whom we prepare for at Advent, such love will never vanish or weaken.

Prayer

Christ of the welcome, we welcome you;
Christ of faithful love, we invite you among us;
Christ of joy and life, make our hearts
    like yours.

Intention for the Day

Hold in your heart today all who find it difficult to believe in God.

Gospel   Mt 15:30–31

Great crowds came to him, bringing with them the lame, the maimed, the blind, the mute and many others, and he cured them, and the crowd was amazed when they saw the lame walking and the blind seeing, and they praised the God of Israel.

Reflection

What attracted so many?

Something about Jesus attracted people to him—his miracles, his compassion, his words, and just who he was. He was the sort of person others liked to be around—unless they were content to live in meanness and in sin. But even then something about him could break through those barriers. If large crowds came to him, would you have been with them?

It is a grace to know Jesus and to love him. Each of us has our favorite aspect of him, as each of us relates in a different way to different friends. As we read the Gospel, we can be attentive to what attracts us—Jesus' kindness, compassion, justice, prayer, or some other aspect. What attracts him to us is a source of our love for him, and a source of life within us. People in the Gospel stories came to him because they needed him. It's the same for us.

Prayer

Christ of the welcome, be close to us.
Nourish us with the bread of life,
feed us with the plenty of God.

Intention for the Day

Hold in your heart today those who have been your teachers in the ways of faith.

Gospel   Mt 7:24

"Everyone then who hears these words of mine and acts on them will be like a wise man who built his house on rock."

Reflection

Foundations in Life

We look for foundations in our lives, upon which to build our decisions, our relationships, our "way of being in the world." Questions like "what are my priorities?" "what do I feel strongly about?" are questions we find addressed in the Gospels; therefore, the Word of God is a foundation for us, offering us a way of life, convictions to live by, something upon which we can stand firmly and live.

In his word, Jesus invites us to know we are loved by God, to work for justice, and to relate to others in compassion and in love. These invitations are unshakable foundations and the Gospel invites us not only to hear them, but to act on them. Each of us can discover the particular words of the Gospel that personally call us to live and act as Jesus' follower.

Prayer

Jesus, way of God, guide us in life.
Jesus, truth of God, enlighten our decisions.
Jesus, life of God, may we know your life to
    the full.

Intention for the Day

Hold in your heart today those who work among the poor.

Gospel   Mt 9:27

As Jesus went on from there, two blind men followed him, shouting, "Have mercy on us, Son of David."

Reflection

Journeying Together

No one can make life's journey alone. The blind men knew that, and many others who came to Jesus also felt their dependency on others. Knowing and accepting another person, in strength and weakness, and being known and accepted yourself brings a certain depth to life and the experience of companionship on life's journey.

At times, all of us need a guide, a shelter, footprints we can walk in. No footprints are more secure than those of Jesus. He guides us to true joy, happiness, and fulfillment. And, unexpectedly, the footprints of others in our lives may be the footprints of Jesus for us. Our restored sight, perhaps received through others, can show us new ways, sure and faithful ways to God in Jesus.

Prayer

Jesus, Son of God and Son of Mary,
   have mercy on us.
Jesus, guide and friend to the twelve,
   have mercy on us.
Jesus, center of the community of the Church,
   have mercy on us.

Intention for the Day

Hold in your heart today those companions, both living and deceased, with whom you have shared your life of faith.

Gospel   Mt 10:7

"As you go, proclaim the good news, 'The kingdom of heaven has come near.'"

Reflection

God Is Near

Advent means God is close, God is near, God is on the way. People and places are environments in which we find God; there can be a "density of the divine" in holy places and holy people of all nations and all faiths.

Advent and Christmas are seasons of the density and the closeness of our God. God is on a journey toward us in Mary and in the Son she is carrying. Is our own journey so fast, so complicated, so rushed that we miss God on God's journey? Perhaps we pass God by like planes in the night sky, anonymous faces on a bus, people mindlessly fighting traffic. But something new can happen for us each Advent, each Christmas, because God makes the journey *anew* symbolized in the simplest way we know: a mother and her child. If only we take the time to realize how near God is.

Prayer

May I bring forth the kingdom of justice,
may I bring forth the kingdom of peace,
may I bring forth the kingdom of God.

Intention for the Day

Hold in your heart today those who work for peace.

Gospel

Mt 3:3

This was what the prophet Isaiah spoke of when he said, "The voice of one crying out in the wilderness: Prepare the way for the Lord, make his paths straight."

Reflection

The Voice of John

John's is a strident voice, contrasting sharply at times with what appears to be the "gentle Jesus of Christmas." John presents a tough message, demanding conversion and change. Yet, he, too, was the one who would preach the forgiveness of sins and would "guide the people in the way of peace."

The message of Jesus is comfort and challenge; both are part of our waiting in Advent. Each year, the birth of the Christ-child comforts us, and enfolds us in the warmth and ease of the love of God. We know also that the life of this child will challenge us to take up our cross, and to believe that in every death there is resurrection, in every harsh experience of life can be found the blessing of God.

Prayer

Guide us, Jesus, in the way of peace,
guide us in ways of forgiveness and tolerance,
for then you guide us in the way of God.

Intention for the Day

Hold in your heart today preachers and teachers.

Gospel Lk 5:20

When he saw their faith, Jesus said, "My friend, your sins are forgiven you."

Reflection

Forgiveness *Is* the Presence of God

Jesus still lives. That's the mystery—in the birth of every child, in the need of every poor person, in the love of every man and woman, boy and girl, every human person for another.

His real presence among us in so many ways is in the context of mystery; we will never know everything about Jesus' presence, but we can live the mystery more deeply year by year, Advent by Advent.

The mystery of Jesus is the mystery of God; we know more than a man in Jesus. We know what God is like, the One who always wants to say, "Your sins are forgiven you." Before forgiveness as well as afterward—and always—God calls us "My friend." And even when we aren't aware of it, whenever we forgive each other, God is present.

Prayer

Jesus, always ready to forgive,
    have mercy on us.
Jesus, always ready to forgive, be close to us.
Jesus, always ready to forgive,
    help us to forgive each other.

Intention for the Day

Hold in your heart today those you need to forgive.

Gospel   Mt 18:12

"If a shepherd has a hundred sheep, and one of them has gone astray, does he not leave the ninety-nine on the mountains and go in search of the one that went astray?"

Reflection

Lost and Found

There are times when we feel lost, and that's when we're glad someone cares for us. We all know time spent in the wilderness—times of bereavement and loss, family breakup, poverty, disappointment, illness, and loneliness. We want to hear compassionate voices in our wildernesses… we need the voice of God and of our faith community, our Church.

God is the Shepherd who cares, bringing us a garment to keep out the cold, the dust of the wild, or the rain and snow—because we are so deeply loved. God's voice is the one voice in our wilderness that never stops calling out to us, and others *are* this voice of God for us, possibly turning our wilderness into a garden. And we, in turn, can be voices of hope for still others through our own care and prayer for each other.

Prayer

Be a voice of hope, Lord Jesus,
an ear that listens, a hand that soothes.
Be with us in our wilderness times.

Intention for the Day

Hold in your heart today caregivers who remain with those in need.

Gospel Mt 11:28

"Come to me, all you who are weary and are carrying heavy burdens, and I will give you rest."

Reflection

Secrets That Burden

All of us carry secrets that burden us. Despite this, there is a love and healing in Jesus that can be found nowhere else, a friendship that never wearies. He never tires of us. Knowing this, can we let our secrets out in prayer? Nothing is too much for him.

The healing we discover in prayer is that we are never condemned. A woman said she always sat in the last pew in church. She felt she belonged there because her marriage had fallen apart and she felt rejected by God. But there are no last pews for Jesus; his love for us is not because we are perfect but because we are who we are. In the words of St. Augustine, God loves us most when we love ourselves least. The invitation is to come to God and rest, especially at the worst times of life.

Prayer

Jesus, gentle God,
  be with me in times of trouble.
Jesus, kindly man,
  be with me in times of stress.
Jesus, Son of Mary, Son of God,
  be close to me always.

Intention for the Day

Hold in your heart today people who suffer from depression.

Gospel   Mt 11:15

"Listen, anyone who has ears!"

Reflection

Attractive Words

Jesus had just compared John the Baptist to Elijah and his hearers were upset. Much of what Jesus says in the gospel is disturbing. There are times when we don't want to hear words like "Forgive your enemies" or "Come, follow me," or words that may challenge something we believe in.

The words of Jesus appeal to the best in us, but are often overshadowed by the worst in us. The call of Jesus is always to a fuller human life, as well as a sincere following in faith. His spirituality is attractive because it is so human and offers a way for the deepest human fulfillment. His message and life, his words about the truth of God, his death and resurrection, will challenge us, just as his birth among the poor makes us question values that are perhaps materialistic. In the midst of this challenge, his friendship and example always help us live what he proposes.

Prayer

Word of Life, teach us truth.
Word of God, teach us about God.
Word made flesh, teach us to be human.

Intention for the Day

Hold in your heart today those who have served as your teachers in life.

Gospel   Mt 11:18–19

"For John came neither eating nor drinking, and they say, 'He has a demon'; the Son of Man came eating and drinking, and they say, 'Look, a glutton and a drunkard.'"

Reflection

Sign of Contradiction

Some people could never be satisfied with Jesus. When he mixed with sinners, they looked down him, but if he had lived a hermit's life and fasted all the time, they still wouldn't have been satisfied. Jesus' compassion and inclusiveness of everyone got under people's skin, and they ridiculed him for the people he loved.

Jesus was always a sign of contradiction, but in such a way that led good people to be better. Only those who wanted no change in their lives opposed him, eventually leading him to death. Even in the first weeks after he came among us, rulers were threatened by news of his birth and little children were killed in his place.

Prayer

Jesus, lover of the poor, give us freedom.
Jesus, lover of the free, give us compassion.
Jesus, lover of the compassionate, give us love.

Intention for the Day

Hold in your heart today the children of your immediate and extended family.

Gospel   Mt 17:12

"So also, the Son of Man is about to suffer at their hands."

Reflection

Looking into the Future

Isn't it strange to know the future of a child? Each time we visit a Bethlehem nativity scene, we can see also the shadow of the cross: the "babe soon to be nailed to a tree." In a short time, the baby born in such poverty and love would demonstrate his love through his death.

We know little of the future when we watch a newborn baby, but we can presume that every life will have its mixture of joy and sorrow, pleasure and suffering. It was no different for God-made-man. In Mary's baby, we touch the full reality of life. We hope for the best for our children, and know that God cares as much for every child as for Jesus. We hope to introduce our children to the knowledge of Jesus with his message of hope for good times and bad.

Prayer

Jesus, Lord of life, give us hope.
Jesus, carrier of hope, give us joy.
Jesus, joy of God, make our hearts like yours.

Intention for the Day

Hold in your heart today parents, your own and those parents you care for.

Gospel   Jn 1:26–27

"I baptize you with water. Among you stands one whom you do not know, the one who is coming after me; I am not worthy to untie the thong of his sandal."

Reflection

The God of the Everyday

We can search for God and for Jesus in many ways and in many places. The people who came to John were looking for "the one who was to come." They may have been looking for someone like John or for a fervent religious leader.

We, too, tend to look for God in dramatic ways—like healing from a terminal illness, great feelings of awe and peace, or in places connected to apparitions. But "the God of the everyday" is the one who is always among us: in the people we meet, in the quiet spaces of prayer, and in our courageous endurance of life's troubles. Our daily living-with-God is a quiet, non-dramatic and gentle awareness that God is near us, among us…even when we do not recognize God.

Prayer
Be with us, Lord, each day, each moment;
may we recognize you in our times of prayer
and in the people we are close to.

Intention for the Day
Hold in your heart today those who have reminded you of God.

Gospel   Mt 21:31

"I tell you, the tax collectors and prostitutes are going into the kingdom of God ahead of you."

Reflection

Beyond Words

Jesus has always looked beyond words to how people act. He judges on people's desires to *do* good and to *be* good, for he knows we do not always succeed. But one of his few condemnations was toward hypocrites. Jesus has little time for the one who promises much and delivers little, whose religion is only words and dogmas with little love and compassion. Maybe he would prefer that we promise only what we know we can deliver, and remain faithful to what we can promise.

Jesus knows that our belonging to God is a gift of God. We belong by living a life of love, strengthened in our goodness and healed in our weakness, always forgiven for sins, faults, and failings. Our waiting for the coming of God increases our faith that we belong to God.

Prayer

Jesus, may love come to birth in us,
may your birth bring hope and joy,
may you be born again in our hope, love,
    and joy.

Intention for the Day

Hold in your heart today those who are victims of abuse.

Gospel   Mt 21:32

"For John came to you in the way of righteousness and you did not believe him but the tax collectors and prostitutes believed him; and even after you saw it, you did not change your minds and believe him."

Reflection

Openness to Faith

Jesus seems to expect faith, and hopes we recognize the truth of his message. Something of the message of the Gospel appeals to the best in human nature: to treat each other with justice, to care for the earth, and to be faithful to the people closest to us. We can be diverted away from the best of human nature by our fears of losing love, security, and comfort, and by the way we can be drawn to sin and selfishness.

When we are weak and vulnerable like people whom society despises—the very people of his time that Jesus befriended—we are sometimes most open to the love and Word of God. Advent can be a time when we deepen our desires for the best in human nature and we become more aware of the ways selfishness can draw us away from God.

Prayer

Open our hearts to know your love,
    Lord Jesus,
open our minds to know your truth,
open our souls to know your love.

Intention for the Day

Hold in your heart today those you know are very poor.

Gospel Lk 7:22

"Go and tell John what you have seen and heard: the blind receive their sight, the lame walk, the lepers are cleansed, the deaf hear, the dead are raised, the poor have the good news brought to them."

Reflection

Knowing God

People are always asking how we know God is present or that God exists. People put the same question to Jesus during his time. And the answer? When we try to heal each other's troubles—listening or just being present with people at bad times—God is present. When we try to work for peace or the betterment of life in our neighborhood, God is near. When we stay faithful to those we are responsible for, God is close. In the practice of real love, God's love is alive.

Even when our own faith feels weak, if we go out to care for and help someone in need, we will find faith and discover that God is near. Our faith grows through the practice of our faith in prayer and action.

Prayer

Jesus, may we see you in the poor,
may we care for you in the ill and the weak,
may we be your love today.

Intention for the Day

Hold in your heart today people who feel hopeless and troubled.

Gospel   Lk 7:27

"See, I am going to send my messenger ahead of you who will prepare your way before you."

Reflection

Personal Message

There is a difference between a message delivered personally and a letter or e-mail message. The personal message provides a chance to see the messenger's mood and to hear his or her tone of voice. God's messengers are always personal. John the Baptist, the messenger of God for Jesus, made an impact that no written message could ever make! The urgency of John's message, the fire in his eyes and the energy in his belly called for real listening. Those who heard could not but react or respond personally, either accepting or rejecting his message. Jesus, as God's Word, was uniquely a personal message of God's love: from his conception to birth to adulthood and to death and resurrection.

Our greatest dignity as a human being is to be aware that we are children of God—then the least in God's kingdom is greater even than John. We are *all* personal messengers of God as we prepare to celebrate the birth of Jesus Christ.

Prayer

May others hear your word in my words,
may others know your love in my presence,
may we all find the presence of your Father
    among each other.

Intention for the Day

Hold in your heart today anyone who has been a personal messenger of God for you.

Gospel   Jn 5:36

"The works that the Father has given me to complete, the very works that I am doing, testify on my behalf that the Father has sent me."

Reflection

Recognizing the Lord

Many people claim to have come from God or have messages from God, or warnings of doom for the world from a heavenly visitor.

Most people are skeptical of such extraordinary statements. And in fact, the fullness of God's message for us has been said in Jesus Christ.

We know that someone is from God by their works. Jesus pointed to his own works of healing, forgiveness, inclusiveness, compassion, death, and resurrection as a way of proving he came from God. It's the same with us: we know we are carriers of God by what we do rather than what we say. When a person lives and acts in love, compassion, and justice, then God is present and coming to birth again in the world.

Prayer

Lord of love, be near us;
Lord of compassion, be merciful;
Lord of justice, be among us.

Intention for the Day

Hold in your heart today religious leaders throughout the world.

Gospel   Mt 1:23

"She will give birth to a son and they shall call him Emmanuel."

Reflection

What's in a Name?

A person's name is important to him or her. We like or dislike our name, we may be glad to be called after someone, or disappointed we don't have a name that seems special. We savor the sound of our name spoken by a loved one. We can be mocked by the way our name is spoken. Our name says something about us— perhaps our parents' hopes or joys are summed up in our name.

It's the same for Jesus. His name, Emmanuel, sums him up for us. The main purpose of his life was to make God present among us, and so his name means "God is with us." He made God truly present in his healing, his listening, his speaking the Word of God, and in his prayer with others. We, too, can do the same. Our second name could be like his: Emmanuel.

Prayer

God, be with us in trouble;
God, be with us in joy;
God, be with us, now and forever.

Intention for the Day

Hold in your heart today everyone you will celebrate the Christmas season with.

Gospel   Mt 1:1

An account of the genealogy of Jesus the Messiah, the son of David, the son of Abraham.

Reflection

Waiting in Hope

The people of Israel waited for years. The Gospel lists generations of people as Jesus' ancestors. Did they tire of waiting, as we may do sometimes? We can get tired of waiting to sense God's closeness in our lives; we can feel angry at God for the rough life we've been dealt. Or we can wonder why God doesn't make peace happen overnight.

The Church makes its Advent prayer: "delay no more." Truthfully, we want fullness of life or peace of mind, and we want it now! Can we make this prayer with faith and trust, aware that we don't know how and when God gives us peace, and aware also that much of our unhappiness in life is caused by the greed and selfishness of others? With faith and trust in God, notwithstanding the urgency of our needs, we wait in hope.

Prayer
Come, Lord Jesus, into our emptiness,
come into our poverty and dependency,
come with your word of joy.

Intention for the Day
Hold in your heart today people everywhere who are most in need of prayer.

Gospel   Mt 1:21

"She will bear a son and you are to name him Jesus, because he will save his people from their sins."

Reflection

Reaching Another

Have you ever seen a person trying to reach something that is out of reach? They stretch their arm to its limit as they try to reach someone who is stuck, or to free an animal trapped in a tree. Every breath and sinew of the body is focused on stretching those last few millimeters.

God's desire to help us is like that, and so we pray to be reached by the outstretched arm of God. Reaching "from heaven to earth," God wants to bring us to life, truth, and love. That is why Jesus comes among us. That kind of love is the beginning of Christmas and the reason for it.

Prayer

Born to Mary, you will be raised by the Father.
Born in poverty, you will be raised in glory.
Come to birth, Jesus, in our love for each other.

Intention for the Day

Hold in your heart today those who cannot spend Christmas with their loved ones.

Gospel   Lk 1:15

"Even before his birth, he will be filled with the Holy Spirit."

Reflection

Carrier of God

Each one of us is loved from "before our birth." As we contemplate the Gospel stories during the days before Jesus' birth, we know that Mary is carrying One filled with the Spirit of God. We can be amazed at this fullness of God in a child, but each and every child is filled with the love of God from the first moment of conception. When a mother carries a child in her womb, and a father leads a child by the hand, they are carrying and leading the small body where God has found a home.

Because of this gift of God's immanent presence, all of us belong in the stable of Bethlehem. In a sense, we have been born there because we are born in the love of God's Spirit as were Jesus and John the Baptist.

Prayer

Jesus, child of God, come to birth in each of us, with the hope, the joy, and the wisdom of God; surround us with your Spirit of new love.

Intention for the Day

Hold all expectant mothers and fathers in your heart today.

Gospel Lk 1:38

"Here am I, the servant of the Lord; let it be done to me according to your word."

Reflection

Goal in Life

Our goal in life gives us a purpose and a meaning. Without it, we are lost in confusion and emptiness. Mary had a great and generous goal in life after the visit from the angel:

her whole life would now be directed toward the birth and mission of her Son. This would make her feel alive and give energy to her body and soul.

We admire a person with a great goal in life, especially when that goal and purpose brings life and care to others. Many have been educated, brought back to health, cared for in old age because of the dedication of people who were servants of the Lord in their service of others.

Prayer

Call me in your love, Lord God,
call me into the service of your people
    and Church,
for I am your servant and will do your word.

Intention for the Day

Hold in your heart today young people trying to decide how best to spend their lives.

Gospel   Lk 1:45

"Blessed is she who believed that there would
be a fulfillment of what was spoken to her by
the Lord."

Reflection

The Joy of Faith

Faith in Jesus is one of the rocks of our lives.
Although Mary's faith endured many "tests"
through the hardships she experienced be-

cause of her Son, today's Gospel story praises Mary for her faith—for believing that what God promised her would be fulfilled.

When we have lived through a time of change in our life, we will generally be most grateful for the love and care we received and gave to one another in friendship. Love is the most fulfilling of all God's gifts, and Mary was blessed with the happiness of believing strongly in God's nearness to her and involvement in her life.

Prayer

Son of Mary, save us.
Son of God, save us.
Brother of us all, save us.

Intention for the Day

Hold in your heart today all who have loved you in life.

Gospel   Lk 1:53

"He has filled the hungry with good things, and sent the rich away empty."

Reflection

Tears of God

God suffers in the suffering of people who are hungry and thirsty, and those who suffer in other ways as well. The prophets spoke about the tears of God as God looked at the world and saw the sufferings of violence and war, of innocent people victimized in many ways.

Jesus spoke of seeing crowds of people who looked like sheep without a shepherd, going the wrong way. This pains God, who wants to save us. God suffers when we suffer, even though we don't understand the suffering of God. God suffers with tears that are tears of action, sending into the world Jesus, Son of God, Son of Mary, to save us from the ruin we can bring on ourselves.

Prayer

Help us delay no longer, Lord God,
in our care for others
and our efforts to build a better world.

Intention for the Day

Hold in your heart today the millions of children throughout the world who are hungry.

Gospel   Lk 1:57

The time came for Elizabeth to give birth and she bore a son.

Reflection

Loving What We Create

We value what we create: a photo, a work of art, a garden. We value the love we create among us, and we especially value our children. Like Elizabeth and Mary, who loved their children "to bits."

We can usually remember how anything we have created began. We remember the beginning of anything we have helped flourish and come to full growth. God, too, remembers when we were nothing and wants to help us develop to our full potential. So we pray with hope that God will help us fulfill our dreams and desires for goodness, for joy, and for love in our life.

Prayer

Create in us, Lord Jesus, hearts and minds
that long for beauty, since you are beauty,
and that long for love, for your name is Love.

Intention for the Day

Hold in your heart today all those who have partici-pated in God's creative work.

Gospel Lk 1:78–79

"By the tender mercy of our God, the dawn from on high will break upon us, to give light to those who sit in darkness and in the shadow of death."

Reflection

In the Shadow of Death

Millions live literally in the shadow of death in war-torn countries. In a free country, we occasionally reawaken to what a gift it is to be able to walk the streets without the danger of explosions, to vote freely in elections, and to live without constant fear for our lives. We are grateful that our children are not enrolled as child-soldiers and can complete their education.

Jesus' first weeks, however, were lived in the shadow of death, as Herod sought to kill him. He shared in the worst of life that we might share in the best of life. The first message of his life is "Peace on earth." May we always hope for this peace, pray for it, and cooperate in whatever way we can in the work of peace. Peacemakers are the privileged ones of God's family.

Prayer

Lead us from despair to hope,
from hate to love,
from war to peace.

Intention for the Day

Hold in your heart today those who work for the poorest of the poor and for peace.

BOOKS & MEDIA

The Daughters of St. Paul operate book and media centers at the following addresses. Visit, call or write the one nearest you today, or find us on the World Wide Web, www.pauline.org

CALIFORNIA
3908 Sepulveda Blvd, Culver City, CA
    90230   310-397-8676
5945 Balboa Avenue, San Diego, CA
    92111   858-565-9181
46 Geary Street, San Francisco, CA
    94108   415-781-5180

FLORIDA
145 S.W. 107th Avenue, Miami, FL
    33174   305-559-6715

HAWAII
1143 Bishop Street, Honolulu, HI
    96813   808-521-2731
Neighbor Islands call: 800-259-8463

ILLINOIS
172 North Michigan Avenue,
    Chicago, IL 60601
    312-346-4228

LOUISIANA
4403 Veterans Blvd, Metairie, LA
    70006   504-887-7631

MASSACHUSETTS
885 Providence Hwy,
    Dedham, MA 02026
    781-326-5385

MISSOURI
9804 Watson Road,
    St. Louis, MO 63126
    314-965-3512

NEW JERSEY
561 U.S. Route 1, Wick Plaza,
    Edison, NJ 08817
    732-572-1200

NEW YORK
150 East 52nd Street, New York, NY
    10022   212-754-1110
78 Fort Place, Staten Island, NY
    10301   718-447-5071

PENNSYLVANIA
9171-A Roosevelt Blvd, Philadelphia,
    PA 19114   215-676-9494

SOUTH CAROLINA
243 King Street, Charleston, SC
    29401   843-577-0175

TENNESSEE
4811 Poplar Avenue, Memphis, TN
    38117   901-761-2987

TEXAS
114 Main Plaza, San Antonio, TX
    78205   210-224-8101

VIRGINIA
1025 King Street, Alexandria, VA
    22314   703-549-3806

CANADA
3022 Dufferin Street, Toronto, Ontario,
    Canada M6B 3T5   416-781-9131
1155 Yonge Street, Toronto, Ontario,
    Canada M4T 1W2   416-934-3440

¡También somos su fuente para libros, videos y música en español!

Don't Let Lent Pass You By…

A Daily Companion for the Season

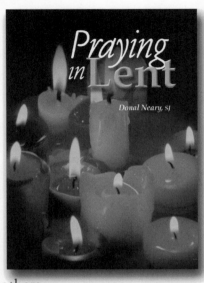

Praying in Lent
Donal Neary, SJ

Lent can so easily pass us by. Space and time made for prayer— however brief—can help deepen our personal faith and our hope in the resurrection of our Lord, bringing about change in ourselves, and ensuring that our lives will benefit others.

Praying in Lent brings the Lenten daily Gospel into focus. It provides insights for linking everyday life with the message of Jesus Christ, and offers suggestions for concrete resolutions to help our prayer become action for others.

#5941-9
paperback, 112 pages
$8.95 ($17.75 Canada)

Pauline
BOOKS & MEDIA
www.pauline.org
800-876-4463